'You have a minute, Lord?'

David Rossoff

This book is for my sons. For Simon, my first-born, for whose quiet strength I am often grateful, and for Paul, who died too young.

By the same author

BIBLE STORIES RETOLD

THE BOOK OF WITNESSES

THE THREE DONKEYS

THE VOICES OF MASADA

THE LITTLE BOOK OF SYLVANUS

'You have a minute, Lord?'

A sort of a prayer book by

David Kossoff

Illustrated by the author

Including the three pieces
'Words for Paul'

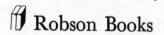 Robson Books

FIRST PUBLISHED IN GREAT BRITAIN IN 1977
BY ROBSON BOOKS LTD., 28 POLAND STREET,
LONDON W1V 3DB. COPYRIGHT © 1977 DAVID
KOSSOFF.

First impression September 1977
Second impression November 1977
Third impression March 1978
Fourth impression December 1978
Reprinted 1980

Kossoff, David
  'You have a minute, Lord?'
  1. Prayer-books
  I. Title
  242'. 8   BV245

  ISBN 0-86051-009-3

Printed in Great Britain by
The Garden City Press Limited
Letchworth, Hertfordshire SG6 1JS

Dirty world

Lord, a word.
It's about the world.
Your world that you made in six days,
   resting on the seventh and being
   pleased with your work.
And rightly so, Lord. It was
   a beautiful world you made.
Beautiful.
Well, Lord, it's getting dirty.
We're dirtying it, Lord.

You made the seas and the creatures
   therein, Lord.
And we are choking the creatures
   with filth and oil, Lord.
You made all the creatures that
   fly and swim and live on land.
And you looked upon them and said, 'Good.'
Well, Lord, there's quite a few
   you wouldn't be able to find.
   Or not recognise if you did find them.
Mutants, Lord. Scientific cross-breeding and such.

Lord, you made us, and from
   our ribs made the rest of us.

And you made us clever, Lord,
  some cleverer than others.
And the *really* clever ones try to
  improve on your work, Lord.
They make a lot of noise,
  And a lot of smoke.
  And a lot of what are called waste-products
  – and (cleverest of all) a lot of what's called
  indestructible refuse.
So we are dirtying up your world, Lord.
  Pollutants, Lord. Effluents and such.

Wonderful gifts you gave us, Lord.
  Riches beyond imagination.
Now we have the fastest roads and
  the fastest cars and the fastest planes.
And we kill ourselves by the thousand.
  In a second; in a pile up; in enormous noise.
  In considerable indignity, Lord.
Three score years and ten if you're lucky, Lord.

Every spring you make it all new again, Lord,
Every summer it all grows.
Every autumn you show us colours to
  catch the breath, to swell the heart.
Every winter you remind us who's Boss.

We need reminding, Lord.
  We litter the place.
  We clash with the colours.
  And worse, to be quite honest, Lord,
  a lot of us *don't notice*.
You forgive a lot of sin, Lord.
  How do you keep your temper with *indifference*?

Too touchy, Lord

Lord, this may be a bit trivial-sounding,
    but if you've got a minute,
I'll come straight to the point; no messing about.
    I'm too touchy, Lord.
    Too touchy by half.
    I see slights and offence where none are meant.
    I hear 'tones' in what people say –
'It's not *what* was said, it was *how*,' and all that rubbish.

Now, Lord, it occurs to me
That being touchy is sort of thinking that
    you (not you, me) ought to be treated in
    some special way,
To allow for the hearing tones and all that.
Which is surely bad, Lord. A sort of sin.
One of the seven or so deadlies.

Or is it the exact opposite?
    A feeling of *un*sureness?
*Over*sensitivity, *in*feriority, *im*maturity?
Either way, it's difficult for people to
    be easy with you (not you, me),
Which is difficult, Lord, for *all* parties.
And certainly for all parties at parties.
That's if I ever get invited.

It may be, Lord, that I'm *not* imagining things
   (here I go again – honestly, I'm a *pain*),
That there *are* 'tones' and nastinesses and slights.
   After all, *I* take up a tone,
   I am nasty, *I* am hurtful.
If I'm right, Lord, let it not affect me so much.
You see, Lord (try to follow this),
   I really *don't* want to do unto others
   As I *imagine* they are doing unto me.

Give it a moment, Lord? At your earliest?

Girlwatching

Lord, these are some thoughts in an aeroplane
   – you have a minute? – about six miles
   up in the sky.
Seems a good time to talk to you, as I'm nearby.
If you don't mind, I'll sort of lead up to
   what I want to ask you about.
Coming straight out with it may be . . .
   kind of . . . if you know what I mean.
And who, let's face it, knows better than you what I
      mean?

So, six miles up. Aeroplane. Not much to do.
   No movie on this flight and I've no book.
Nothing to look at except the stewardesses.
   And worth the trouble, Lord (I'm an expert).
One blonde and smiling, blue-eyed,
   the other grave and dark.
They move and turn and stretch and bend,
   a pas de deux of infinite variety and harmony.
Quite unaware of the pleasure they give,
   to me, a lifelong girlwatcher.

Girlwatching, Lord. The subject of our talk.
The feasting of the eyes; the constant
   appreciation of the miracle you wrought
   with one borrowed rib.

A tempter of Adam, yes;
    of all Adams since, yes,
But a marvellous invention, Lord.
On behalf of all Adams, our sincere thanks.
    Six miles up or at ground level,
    our sincere thanks.

There are many kinds of Girlwatching, Lord,
About as many as there are kinds of men.
    Ranging from the groaning 'Caw . . !'
    to the 'Handsome filly, what?'
From the look of wide-eyed wonder,
To the hooded swift undressing piercer.
    From the Sonnets to the psalms,
    from Solomon's Songs to porn.
Lord, what made Adam look, made Rubens look.
And Rembrandt and Titian and Byron,
    and Hefner and Pirelli, and me.

Anything wrong in it, Lord? Sometimes I worry.
Girlwatching found me a good wife, but
    marrying her in no way ended the habit.
Homemaking, fatherhood, breadwinning,
    career-building, all made room for it.

Later, older, more academic, a lengthy
    research in Biblical matters and related
    religions didn't stop it for a minute.
Nothing stops it. Not care nor concern nor
    sadness nor irritation nor illness – not even
    funerals, Lord.
Black does nice things for a woman . . .
Anything wrong in it, Lord?
Surely not. After all, that man should be
    attracted to a woman was *your* idea.
Good thinking, dear Creator.

True Girlwatching, Lord, the real stuff,
    rarely initiates any action in the matter.
It should stir the imagination, not the loins,

The delight is for the eyes alone.
Lust clouds the vision, and should have no place.
A distinguished Watcher of my acquaintance
   once said: 'To be near enough to touch
   or to smell perfume or to see the artifice
   of make-up is too near. An exchange
   of words, too, has its dangers and should
   be avoided. One should Watch from a
   little way off.'
A longish quote, Lord, but I thought you
   might be interested.
Anything wrong in it, dear Friend?

These thoughts high in the sky, Lord,
   are prompted not just by the desire to
   give thanks on behalf of all Adams,
Not just to show gratitude for the so-close-
   to-Heaven pas de deux,
But to say again how much I
   appreciate what you do for me.
Girlwatching could only have been given
   by you, dear Friend. The Adams didn't make
   it up, any more than they made anything else
   without your help.
And, older now, I see thy infinite wisdom.
   For Girlwatching is a solace, Lord.
   A comfort, a joy, a gift, a harmless delight.
Which warms the eye and soul of a man
When his other fires are dying a little . . .

The youth

You have a minute, Lord? Or maybe two?
For this may take a while to get the words right.
Well, it's the youngsters, Lord.
'The youth' as the papers call them.
A funny looking lot, it can't be denied.
Walking free, uninhibited
  – except that they all seem to be
  walking in step, Lord.
All uninhibited in the same rather
  inhibited way.
Are they (I'll keep my voice low, Lord) *conforming*?

Leave that for a minute, though;
  you still there, Lord?
Look at us grown-ups, Lord – and weep.
Seems we're not so clever either.
We comfort ourselves that we do our best
  for our kids.
Try to show them (in ourselves) a good example.
But nearly all the grown-ups *I* know, Lord,
Don't know their arse (you should excuse me) from
  their elbow.
An example? Us? Oh boy.

Lord, help us to remember we were also
  young once – and that we almost

certainly *were* like that at their age.
Stop us being *stuffy*, Lord.
It's a great bore to all concerned.
Help us recall (unexpurgated) the
    things *we* got up to.
We also tried out new sensations, Lord,
    also looked funny (to our elders),
    also gave our parents worry.
Kids do; they just do.

Lord, I'll come to the point.
What worries me most (like most grown-ups)
Is what's going to become of the kids.
But (confidentially) what worries me nearly as much,
Is that a lot of 'em are going to become like us.
Full of disapproval for the kids
    of *their* grown-up time.
Full of head-shakings – and cleverly
    edited stories of what *they* were like.
Full of non-comprehension and
    (worse) 'I don't wanna know.'

So Lord, help me to learn a little from the kids.
    And by knowing that bit more,
Maybe they'll think *me* worth learning from.
You see, Lord (of *course* you see),
    older is not necessarily wiser,
Not in the matter of understanding kids.
    Teach me to comprehend,
    for, believe me, I *do* wanna know.

Vandals, Lord

Lord, may I bring up another little
   something?
   You have a minute?
It's a little something which I don't
   really understand; makes me
   very mad; and is very common.
Vandalism, Lord.
The religion of the Spoilers.
The Defacer Sect. The Initial Carvers.
The Breakers-off of Bits. The Wall-Writers.

You know, Lord, despite the community
   hymn-singing before the game, and
   the fervent thanks to you after, I've
   never had the impression that you
   have any great interest in football.
I may be wrong; never mind.
Well, lately it occurs to me that it
   may be supporters you're not keen on.
Not all of 'em; some.
Those who go on rampage through
   the away towns and break up the
   train on the way home
And after smashing all the lavatories
   make their own W.C. arrangements.

I'm a bit of a sightseer, Lord.
  A visitor of ancient places, of
  well-kept ruins, preserved sites.
Places of keeps and graceful towers
  and age-old galleries and woodwork
  full of memory ...
Mainly full of memory of past
  sightseers whose initials, names,
  addresses and messages are on every
  available surface.
Often carved with great care; deeply
  and carefully; taking time.
Statues to themselves, Lord?
Can't you get 'em on a
  'graven images' charge?

A psychiatrist friend of mine, Lord,
  once came to dinner and dwelt
  calmly and at some length upon
  the reasons for vandalism.
Learned chap; long words; retained
  by a number of film stars.
Explained the whole thing. Twice.
Said his goodnights with grace and
  charm. Hand-kiss for all the ladies.
Left, and was back within the minute,
  screeching;
Persons unknown had inscribed his
  Bentley with a pub dart.

Another pal of mine, Lord,
  Nearly lost his wife and unborn
  son (very premature) on the same night.

No 'phone at home so off he ran.
All four call boxes in his district
  had been done by the Spoilers,
The Breakers-off of Bits.
Do you make a note of their names, Lord?
Please do for your own sake.
  For, believe me, if you soften and
  let 'em in, they'll smash the place up.

No hiding place, Lord, they get everywhere.
No place is safe from the Sect.
  Reinforced concrete and stainless
  steel do in no wise deter them.
They call in the affiliated unions;
The Initiallers, the Wall-writers (in
  indelible paints), the Window-
  scorers, the Toilet-smashers, the
  Grand Federation of Destruction.
Railings do not their resolution fade
Nor iron bars their rage.

For rage is in it, dear Friend.
He of the inscribed Bentley said so.
  But before we return to him,
  a word about the type of
  vandalism that really makes my
  pale blues see red.
Churches, Lord. Or *any* place of worship.
  (I'm not sucking up, honest. Indeed
  the feeling of outrage is more aesthetic
  than religious – I hope you don't mind.)

I've been in churches, old beautiful
   churches, where there just isn't
   room to scratch another name.
Unless you scratch out someone else's
   from, say, Nebraska, to dig in your
   own, from Liverpool.

On centuries-old doors do they scratch and dig,
On the pews, the paving and the pulpit.
   On gravestones and tombs.
   On the walls of spiral stairways to
   the bell tower – and on the bells themselves.
On the windows do they leave their mark.
On ancient painted screens.
   The font gets a word or two,
   the altar also.
   Choir stall, very popular. Like the organ.
An idea for the punishment, Lord!
   (Only a suggestion, of course.)
Your initials, dug with a blunt nail,
   on *their* organ.

Back to he of the Bentley, Lord, and
   of his talk about rage.
Yes, it makes sense; everybody stores
   up desires to hit back, to break
   things, to show 'em.
Easier to cut up a bus seat than cut
   up your teacher, or your mum.
More satisfying to push in a shop window
   than your father's stupid face.
Rage, pent-up anger, long-nurtured.
   Resentments, frustration, repression.
What an atom-pile of energy is there.

Another minute, Lord?
Must all that energy be destructive?
It could move mountains, build great
cities, grow food to feed the world.
It could make, with a little help, peace.
Is it too late, Lord, to make a little adjustment?
To redirect all that vast energy?
It may be that having made us, and
having seen us grow clever enough to
think that *we* made us, you've
become a little weary of us.
It's understandable.
But if, at some future date, we deserve
to catch your interest again,
A little adjustment?

Pausing

A moment, Lord – you have a minute?
A word or two, a sort of despairing wish,
Written high up on a quiet mountain
    looking down across a silent lake.
An April day, cool, now and then warm.
A lot of new greens – and a lot of browns where
    the gorse and trees are still asleep.
So quiet, Lord, so still.

Not much birdsong. A little; far off, far below.
The birds swoop and play and show off,
    but quietly, keeping their voices down.
As though they know my thoughts,
    and want to share the moment.
I'll be honest, Lord, the moment
    is not tremendous, unique, special.
Neither are my thoughts any that I've
    not had before.

But the place and the quietness and
    the feeling of time passing more quickly.
These things together fuse the moment and the
    thought into a resolve to say a word or two.
Funny how I know you are busy
    yet I know you make time to listen.
Make time again, dear Friend, it's important.

Lord, teach me how to stand still.
  To switch off; to lean on a gate;
  to sit and look at your beautiful world.
Teach me how to leave the 'phone off,
  to slacken speed, to lie in the sun without
  a feeling that I should be *doing* something.
Teach me, Lord, to *stop, to stop fussing,*
To stop working at it, to stop keeping on bravely,
To stop doing it all myself ('no help
  y'know, all by myself').

Teach me Lord, to let others help me.
Teach me to delegate, to trust.
That which I do, let's face it, is
  not so important.
Doing it alone makes me *feel* important.

It also makes me feel tired and
  irritable and anxious and fearful
  of what will happen if I'm off sick.
And not liking the thought that very little
  would happen; that the earth would
  not shake – and probably nobody would
  notice for a week or two.
Why can't I stop running, Lord?

Teach me, Lord, to stop, and look, and listen.
  To be still in the mind when I stop.
  To see beauty when I look.
  To hear more when I listen.

Shy children

Lord – you have a minute?
This is a little important. I've been
    meaning to bring this up for some
    weeks, but you know, this and that . . .
It's on behalf of shy children.
I was one, and my eldest is one.
My wife is still one. So's my
    married sister – and my friend Lou.
Lou says to be shy is to remain a
    child in the most painful way.
No fool, Lou.

But let's stay with children, Lord.
Shy grown-ups can cope; in various ways.
    A person learns how. How to
    build the various walls for
    hiding behind. A person learns.
But children, Lord. They have it rough.
And they are surrounded by grown-ups
    who, in the main, don't understand.
Or have forgotten, behind their walls,
    the Hell it can be.

I've read learned bits by educated parties
    positively proving that shy ones
    are made, not born.

Or is it born, not made?
You think it makes any difference, Lord?
You think it's comfort, Lord?
You think it helps a head-bent,
    tongue-tied, blushing, speechless kid?
Like a second head it helps.
Like a third leg.

You should excuse me, Lord,
    but a person could get puzzled.
I'll try to explain.
    A grown-up misbehaves; does wrong;
    breaks one of your ten rules.
You find a way to teach him a lesson, to
    punish him a little.
It's your way; justice with mercy.
Good system. Tried and trusted.

The punishments are graded; as is right.
Ranging from a little slap for a
    little sin to real Hell for a big 'un.
Real Hell. Something as bad as, for
    instance, suddenly making a
    person shy.
Not grown-up shy; with walls.
Shy like a child.
That's real Hell, Lord. Ask a shy child.

So why children, Lord?
Punishment in advance?
Doesn't seem like you – and shy
    people are *less* likely to get into
    big trouble, am I right?
So why children, Lord?

What's the *point* of shyness?
Modesty, yes, sense of proportion, yes.
Quietness, respect for others, yes.
But shyness?
Tongue-locked, brain-blocked,
Turned-in, turned off,
Eye-lowered, head-lowered *Hell*?

Forgive me, Lord, I always seem
   to be raising my voice.
But you are busy; a lot to look after,
   and perhaps things get overlooked.
I don't know how good your staff is.
   (Angels strike me as decorative
   rather than useful. I may be
   wrong. Bit unworldly they seem.)
So things perhaps are not brought
   to your attention.
Well, Lord, you yourself invented the
   way to bring things to your attention,
And called it prayer.
This is a prayer, dear Friend,
   on behalf of shy children.

Loneliness

You have a minute, Lord?
I want to bring up the subject of loneliness.
Not just the kind you get when you're
    on your own. The other kind; that
    never leaves you at all, ever.
The shadow that stands by your side in
    crowded places, and at dinner parties
    with old friends, sits close.

That shadow dilutes living, Lord.
    It waters everything down.
It's got a lot of long names, Lord.
Invented by a lot of real cleverdicks.
Like Acute Depression. (Over Iceland? Over *me*!)
Or Weltshmerz. (Sounds like cheese, Lord.)
Schizoid. (A plastic, Lord?)
Paranoia. (A climbing plant?)

And for all the funny names, Lord,
The cleverdicks have got funny treatments.
    They listen, whilst you, if you've got the
    money, talk. For hours. Even if, as is
    most likely, you are a bore.
    As shadow-owning people mostly are.
Maybe that's why it's costly. Understandable.

Funny though; you lying down, chatting
away, wide awake, and them sitting up,
listening, sleepy.
Or they wire you up and plug you in and
push a switch and give you for nothing
what in America you get only for murder.
(They *like* doing it, Lord.)

They sit you in a ring with others
to pour it all out and find out
you're not the only one.
(You knew that before you sat down.)
They get you making rugs or
assembling things or painting.
Even painters and rugmakers and thing-assemblers.
They have things call Barbiturates.
Barbiturates. (Haircutting speeds, Lord?)
And Sublimation. (Underground floodlighting?)
And Rorshachs. (Big noisy fish? Roar sharks? Ah well.)

Lord, you've probably noticed I can keep up
the bad jokes almost indefinitely.
Others have noticed too; I'm well avoided.
But it's sort of whistling in the dark, Lord,
keeping the old spirits up,
trying to forget the old shadow.

Dear Friend, *you* don't need telling.
The little jokies help.
A fellow I know once said: 'Become a
harmless lunatic; it's the only way to live.'
Was he talking, in despair, about jokies, Lord?

Maybe the cleverdicks *do* know, maybe
  their 'causes' and 'derivations' are right.
But lonely is lonely, Lord, and there's a
  great many of us. A multitude.
Help us, Lord.
If it's because we are 'too turned in',
  turn us inside out,
If it's to do with fear of others,
  give us courage.
If with recall of early rebuff,
  give us bad memories.
If, Lord, it's just because we are
  that sort of person,
Change us.
For pity's sake, for Heaven's sake, change us.
'Cos it's no life, Lord, it's no life.

Must a person suffer fools, Lord?

I've been thinking about stupidity, Lord.
  You have a minute?
Not my own. I avoid thinking too much
  about my own; I get depressed.
No, the kinds of stupidity I meet that
  make me go tetchy and acid.
  Or worse, tense with *un*spoken insult.
Must a person suffer fools, Lord? *Must* he?
Is it so written in the Book?
I'll be honest, Lord. I can't do it.

You made us all. Of infinite variety.
You gave us the vast magics of heredity
  and resemblance and blood groups
  and genetic patterns and 'just-like-his-father'.
A sort of 'I'll make Adam and Eve and
  they can make the rest'.
So it follows that in the infinite
  variety there must be a fair number
  of people who will drive a fair
  number of other people round the bend.
Part of thy glorious plan, Lord?
Thy Inscrutable Blueprint?

Alright. Let me grow not lippy. Let
  me wax not disrespectful.

If the suffering of fools is part
  of the teaching of tolerance, good.
If the patience with idiots maketh
  a person better, also good.
But let me tell you, Lord, the tolerance
  and patience is most of the time
  wasted on the fools and idiots!
I'm not joking – indeed not, it's
  a serious matter – honest!
A person could spit.

Who needs 'em? Who seeks 'em out?
  You gave to me (and indeed I
  thank you) a certain sympathy of nature.
So people talk to me.
Too much and often for too long.
Most of the time I don't mind,
It is a gentle cross to bear.
  (I ought to put that differently
  perhaps, forgive me, but
  you know me well enough
  to know what I'm on about.)
My father used to say, 'Have time for people.'
He had time for people, my father,
  bless his sweet memory. Does
  he keep well, Lord? Give him my love.

A person *should* have time for people.
My father said so and so do you.
But *all* people, Lord? *All*?
  The bigoted, the ignorant, the intolerant,
  the small-minded, the envious, the
  self-centred, the vain, the patronising,

the phoney, the wicked?
Must I, Lord?
If I must, perhaps not so gentle a cross ...
I must tell you, dear Friend, that
   the 'must I?' is rhetorical; an academic question.
For frankly, already admitted, I can't.

No. Wait. You've shown me often enough
   that 'can't' is the talk of children.
The words of no faith. I have faith; I believe.
Help me, Lord, to suffer fools – and
   all those included in the foregoing list.
Help me keep my temper and not use
   my ice-voice and to avoid bad
   language. (Can I punch the occasional eye?)
Help me be patient and bite back insult
   and avoid argument with the stupid
   bastards. (Sorry, Lord, it slipped out.)
I'll try. Help me, I'll try.

Charity

Lord – you have a minute? – a word or
    two about charity.
Possibly a slightly uncharitable word or two.
Forgive my sour note, Lord, it comes from
    a close acquaintance with the subject.
Not so much the true charity of forgiveness
    or tolerance or loving-kindness,
Or the charity that dwells in understanding
    and humour and sympathy.
No, Lord, I speak of giving to Charity;
    the old Fund-raising; the actual parting
    up with real money.

Old campaigner, me, Lord. Appeal-speaker,
    giver of addresses for causes; opener of
    fêtes and coffee mornings; alms-gatherer.
Trained and honed by experts, Lord.
Taught by them (cold-eyed business-like
    fellers, Lord) to keep the eye on the target-figure;
    the end – and not to get too upset about the means.
Not too easy at first, the not getting upset.
'Why they give,' said the cold-eyed men, 'is
    their business. How much they give is ours.'
Cynical and wise in the ways of men, my
    mentors in the raising of cash.

'Observe vanity,' they said, 'and suppress distaste.
   Play it like a fish – and land it.'
'For people,' they said, 'not all, but many, give
   for reasons which have nothing to do with charity.'
'Observe rivalry, and jealousy,' they said, 'and
   keeping up with the Joneses, and Birthday-
   Honours hunters – and take the money.'
Pardon the cynicism, dear Friend (sometimes
   I think a balanced cynicism is the only
   possible attitude of mind).
It provides a little armour for a person.

Self-interest, Lord. The rarity of the truly
   'for others' action.
That I suppose is what I'm talking about.
Two quotes (you have another second or two?):
   'If I was put on this world to help others,
   why were the others put on?'
And the second: 'I don't mind doing a bit of
   good. It makes me feel good – and may do *me*
   a bit of good.'
Both acceptable, Lord, both a bit funny.
Both very 'human'.
But *I* should tell *you* about humans?
You invented 'em.

So, Lord, I'll come to the point.
Teach me, Lord, to give for the right reasons,
   to give freely, with gratitude for all I've
   been given by you.
Let me, Lord, be a giver, not a taker.
   Faith, I have. Hope, I've never lacked.
   But the greatest, I'm told, is Charity.

Lyric for a musical

Lord, you have a minute?
I want to talk about show-business.
All my life I've believed that you
    know everything that goes on.
    All-seeing, all-knowing and so on.
But oddly I've never thought you
    bothered too much with what films
    or plays we go to. What books we read.
I've never thought of you as interested
    in sport, or television.
I may be wide of the mark. Still.

Lord, you know about musicals?
    Musical plays? Plays with music?
Well, lately, they've changed a little.
They used to be about poor-gets-rich
    and boy-loses-girl and boy-gets-girl
    and cowboys and sailors and just
    about every damn (pardon) thing.
Well, lately, there's been one or two
    about your son.
Very polite; nothing nasty; big box-office.
Very respectful; done with taste; expensive seats.

Now, Lord, all this is not to bring the
    matter as it were to your attention:

After all, you made us all – even the critics,
  which would suggest you have
  some knowledge of such things.
No, this is about how such shows
  set the mind working.
I don't mean they convert (although
  they could) or inspire (likewise)
  or show a way (I hope so).

Take me, for instance.
I'm no composer; can't read music
  or play an instrument.
But musicals start lyrics in my mind.
Words start to form.
  (Are psalms lyrics, Lord?)

Lord, this is a bit of a liberty and
  one can lose friends this way
But would you care to hear a lyric?
  You have a minute?

It goes like this. Eight bars intro for
  the disc jockey to make remarks
  over, and straight in:

    Oh there's people killin' people
      And settin' folks alight,
    Yeah there's bombers bombing children
      Too young to read or write –
    Forgive them, Lord, forgive them,
      For they know just what they do.

And there's grown-ups sending schoolboys
    Marchin' off to fight,
And there's churches full of preachers
    Sayin' everybody's right –
Forgive them, Lord, forgive them,
    For they know just what they do.

Now the guys who make munitions,
    Make 'em good; take a pride.
And to show they're democratic,
    They sell to *any* side –
Forgive them Lord, etc.

Insert here Lord, a bit of up-tempo
    on drums, brass, horns and
    organ. Then, with singing group:

Oh forgive them, yeah forgive them,
  Oh forgive them if you can,
For remember, Lord, remember,
  It was you who made a man.
(*No offence, Lord.*) *Last verse:*

Now when a feller kills a feller,
  He's real wicked, through and through,
But when thousands wipe out thousands
  They offer thanks, Lord . . . to you.

So forgive them, Lord, forgive them
  (*Big finish; brass and wood-wind*)
For – they – know – just – what – they
  Do – oo – oo – oo – oo.

If, Lord, you hear from a composer
  stuck for some words,
Remember me?
Even if not . . . remember me?

Young mind

I have been giving thought, Lord
   - you have a minute? - to getting old.
Natural enough, as the years pass.
Do the years pass more quickly, Lord?
Whatever happened to those longer
   years we used to have?
Did you discontinue them? To speed up
   the process, sort of? To replace us faster?
Hoping for improvement in the product?
Understandable.

However, getting old. Subject for today
   - and I'm *not* talking about staying young.
Indeed not; I was young once and
   wasn't mad on it. But to continue.
Getting old, a fellow said, is all in the mind.
True. It's also inclined to get into the joints,
   the digestion, and the poor old feet.
Spectacles appear, then a second pair.
Certain powers wane. Expected; allowed for.
But the fellow's right, or nearly right.

Now, Lord. To the point.
What if the *mind* gets stiff in the joints?
   Where are you then?

What if the *mind* goes lame, needs two
    pairs of specs?
Then, it would seem, a person's got trouble.
I mean, if the mind is in charge, and
    starts taking days off; loses grip.
    Where are you then?
Seems it's time for a person to shut the office.

So, Lord, please, keep me young in the mind.
    Let me enjoy, Lord, let me enjoy.
If creaky I must be, and many-spectacled,
    and morning-stiff and food-careful,
If trembly-handed and slow-moving and
    breath-short and head-noddy,
I won't complain. Not a word.
If, with your help, dear Friend, there
    will dwell in this ancient monument,
A Young Mind. Please, Lord?

Far-from-home terrors

Far from home am I, Lord, with bad toothache.
In the waiting-room of a strange Dentist.
  In a strange town am I, Lord. In pain.
  And in a bad state of plain ordinary fright.
  You have a minute? *Please*?

My own man, Lord, is in Harley Street.
  In some splendour. Fresh-from-the-
  laundry copies of *Punch* and *Country Life*.
  Knee-deep carpet and a receptionist in
  a white coat, with blue hair.
In Harley Street, in splendour, in a big way
  of business and, at present, in Bermuda.

This waiting-room is lino-tiled, Lord, and
  has seven chairs and a table in plastic
  and steel. One notice; one picture; one light.
No one here but me. I've got the shakes, Lord.
The lady outside (normal colour hair) said
  the Dentist will be back soon.
She didn't say from where, Lord. Sinister.
She fitted me in, Lord; emergency; urgent;
  without appointment. But sinister.

In the Far North am I, Lord, where the
  accents are as hard as the landscape.

Hard people. Used to poverty and hardship
and hunger-marches and disasters.
No sympathy for my toothache here, Lord.
Frankly, I'd be afraid to mention it.
They'd laugh. Call me coward.
As though I don't know.

Let the Dentist be from somewhere else, Lord.
Some quiet sympathetic place in the South.
Let him be of gentle upbringing, of
good family, with loving parents.
Let him be married, in perfect happiness,
with lovely children and no mortgage.
Let him enjoy perfectly matched sex with
his beautiful wife (who adores him).

Make thou his hands steady, Lord,
And his breath sweet.
(Funny how Dentists don't use their
own mouth-wash, Lord.)
Make thou his skill complete, his
eye keen and his reading up-to-date.
Where *is* he, Lord? What's *keeping* him?
Let him not make bad jokes, Lord, or
ask me questions when my wide-open
mouth is full of his tools.
Let his tools sit easy in his hand, Lord, and
his hand be easy with the needle.
(Let me not need the needle, Lord.)
But, most important, Lord, let him be *nice*.

I heard the outer door bang, Lord!
Forgive me my trespasses and I will

try to love my neighbour and lift up
mine eyes unto the hills from whence
cometh my help ...
(In fact as long as help comes I'm not
particular from whence it comes.)
I can hear voices, Lord!
... thy rod and thy staff support me ... and
walk with me through the Valley of the
Shadow. Thou art my Shepherd ...
What am I saying?
The voices have stopped, Lord ...

Autumn banquet

Some three or four times in my life, Lord,
    – you have a minute? – it has been my good fortune
To drive all day, across or up or down a well-wooded
    small country, on that one day of the year in autumn,
With the leaves still on, when the colours take
    away the breath and make the heart sing its
    thanks to you, beloved Creator.
The world glows and burns – and round every
    corner you show yet a new colour-miracle.

I drive slowly, for to rush such a meal is
    a swine-like sacrilege. And many-coursed
    is the banquet offered.
The delicate ferns and gorses for starters; the
    late flowers.
Then, for soup, or fish, the smaller trees
    by streams, or away on hills, fringing fields.
Yellows and golds and fawns and pale brown.
I drive on, waiting for the main course,
    taking my time, trusting my Chef.

Now it comes. And, most generous of
    hosts, you offer remarkable, Heavenly choice.
A green plain and a mighty rise of timbered
    mountain, to the sky, of a million trees,

Of many kinds, to offer the full spectrum,
    the whole colour-card – the works!
Then, for change, a long tunnel to float
    through, sun-dappled, faery-gladed.
The leaves, full-grown, of marvellous ambers
    and jades and emeralds. Tunnel of jewels.

I went to a trade school, Lord, where poetry
    was not offered (plumbing was) and 'Scripture'
    was unknown (joinery prepared one better
    for 'the world outside').
Good science and biology department; sound
    Darwinian fellers. Had all the answers.
    The earth had no mysteries for them.
Who gave us the earth was never mentioned.

Want to hear a little joke, Lord? Just
    remembered, just come to mind?
It goes thus. The Instructor in Stress-strain
    Mechanics of Timber used to do marvellous
    blackboard drawings, in many colours.
As, absorbed, he did them, he used to
    whistle softly, through his teeth.
Always the same old song, beloved of
    end-of-pier tenors,
    from which comes the line:
'But only God can make a tree.'

How do you condole, Lord?

Something on my mind, Lord,
   you have a minute, maybe two?
It's about condolence.
I'm not good at it.
I feel; I'm not afraid to show tears.
   I cry easy; I'm sad for the party.
How do you condole, Lord?
   I feel; but the words don't come.

After all, there aren't all that many
   words you can use, Lord;
Death is a clearly defined and
   definite subject, Lord.
Positive; end of chapter; the
   only certainty; must come.
And if it comes before the end of
   the chapter, Lord, there are
   even less words.

Difficult for a person.
   Say you're sorry? Of course you are.
Or if secretly you're *not* sorry
   – you can't *say* it!
If the party, by dying, is freed from
   a life that's no life, it's simpler.

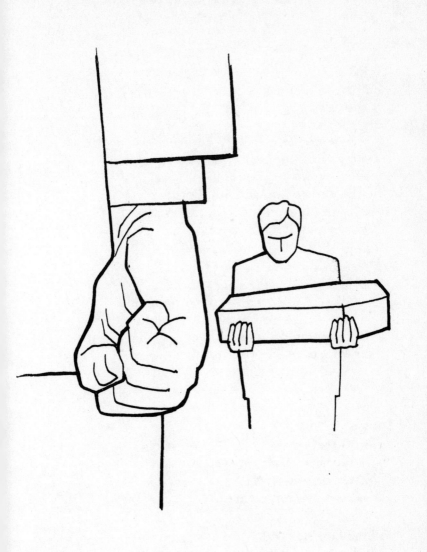

But what do you say to the family of a teenage
    handsome or beautiful party cut
    off in mid-breath?

What are the right words, Lord,
For the early death of good men
    with lots more to give?
For the end of young mothers
    – or young fathers?
Crabby old senile parties are easy;
    a few words on a card.
But buxom young grannies, Lord?
Choir-boys in overturned outing-coaches?
A-level youth-leaders sea-sunk?

What can a person *say*, Lord?
Is it all thy will being done, Lord?
Or did your attention wander for a minute?
One doesn't like to question, Lord, but
    the question comes up. Often.
And what can a person *say*?
To talk of your 'mysterious ways' and
    your 'plan beyond our understanding' is
    no great comfort, Lord.

Not to the parents of an eight-year-old
    beauty with a bloom even in death
    like a perfect peach.
What can you *say*, Lord?

I'll be honest, Lord.
I feel anger. Not against you, dear Friend,

But I hate waste – and I don't like not
  being able to *do* something.
I use (I'm sorry) bad language; I bang
  things with my fist; feel hot, dry-eyed.
Am I wrong, Lord? With the anger?
I'm not the only one.
  A person can't help it.

A thought occurs, Lord – please, another minute?
  And it's not (believe me) a criticism.
It may be that in the running of your
  'ways and plans', the 'selection for
  death' is done by a special
  department up there,
Trained personnel; specialists;
Leaders, who go away on courses.
Well, could they, do you think, be
  getting out of hand?
Doing things without your initial?

I bring this up, Lord,
Because every now and then, let me tell
  you, although I'm sure I've already
  made the point,
It doesn't make too much sense.
You invented sense, Lord.
  Gave us reason, logic, the power
  of two and two.
But when it just *doesn't* make sense, Lord,
What can a person *say*?

One last question, Lord, a final thought,
Does Satan still have a say?

He exists. Evidence to every side.
  Even that in some areas he's winning,
  Or if not ahead, certainly doing well.
Well, does *he* select for death, Lord?
Is it *his* hand sometimes?
  That makes a sort of sense, Lord.
  A sad sort of sense.

Well, I've had my say.
To you I can always speak.
  The words come easy.
  Often you're the only one I *can* talk to.
A great relief; a great peace.
But Lord – and I don't want to be
  a nag – what about the parties
  referred to in the foregoing?
What can a person say to *them*?

Old Sulky

Lord, you have a minute?
This is about sulking. People sulking.
Well, to be honest, Lord, not people; me.
I sulk, Lord.
I go silent and black-thoughted;
Become glowering and covered in frowns and lines.
And nobody suffers but me.

Teach me to laugh it off, Lord.
It's important, honest.
Teach me to get over it faster,
To be normal (whatever *that* is)
   and have a sense of proportion.
Not a lot to ask, Lord.
Sulking is living in a dark room,
   in the wrong spectacles, in a draught.
And if people are nice to you, Lord,
   and 'cope' with you,
You feel ten times worse.

Sulking magnifies its own cause, Lord.
Is a fairground mirror looked into
   with eyes of distorted gaze.
You can't win, it's ridiculous.
Help me win, Lord, help me not be ridiculous.

To tell you the truth, Lord (and I try to),
 I often don't care much one way or
 the other about the things I sulk over.
How silly can a man get?

But you made us, Lord.
You made us fat and thin and tall and short;
Dark and fair, and of many colours.
And it follows that we owe to you the brains
 and the feelings and the senses.
Everything we owe to you.
The sulks too, Lord?
A mistake, Lord? A slip-up?
Who needs sulks, Lord?
 What *good* are they?
What does being sulky *do* for a person, Lord?
Look into it, Lord?
At your earliest convenience?

The other feller is wrong

This, Lord, written in Northern Ireland.
You have a minute?
Make a minute, Lord.
For there are a great many people in
   this sad, sad country who think you
   haven't cast a glance this way in
   half a century.
Sad, sad country.
Where people who worship you in one way
Kill others who worship you in another.

You gave us life, Lord, and brains, and
   a beautiful world to live in.
Six good days' work you did.
   And the work pleased you.
You looked upon your work, the Book says,
   and it pleased you.
'Good,' you said. 'Go multiply,' you said.
And when we'd multiplied and started to
   play up, you gave us the Ten Major
   Rules and a lot of stuff in smaller print.
'Good,' we said. 'Now we know the way.'

Brains you gave us, Lord, to comprehend the Rules.
   To interpret them, to translate them
   into a way of life.

Seems it began to get confused at that
point, Lord.
Started to cloud up. Started to go wrong.
Different interpretations, you see.
Conflicting translations.
Everybody sure that they had it right
and the other feller was wrong.
The Book says you knew, Lord. It says you
got cross, and meted out punishments.

Why did you let it go on at all, dear Friend?
We were your idea; you made us, top
to toe, brains and senses.
Brains enough to interpret and translate,
And know without doubt that we had it
right and the other feller was wrong.
And because it was the Rules, your wishes,
the Word of God, we were arguing about,
Argument became inadequate,
And the killing started. And hasn't stopped.
Why did you let it go on?

Millions have died 'defending their faith',
Killed by others, defending theirs.
And both sides were right; with you on their side.
And upon victory, sacrifices and offerings to you
as a matter of course. As is only right.
Millions dead. On a question of interpretation.
Teach me to understand, Lord.
Let me understand why you permit the
interpreters to foul up what was clear
in the first place.

Lend another minute, Lord, for I am troubled in
  the mind and the words don't come.
These clever ones who tell us what you really
  mean are adults, grown-ups,
Often very persuasive parties, with followers
  and rich patrons and mailing lists of widows
  eager to offer their mites.
But what they are really saying, Lord, is that
  they are right and the other feller is wrong.
Very positive, Lord, some of them.
  Very worrying.

A person can get confused, Lord.
  Is it all part of your great plan?
A sort of Tower of Babel?
  Many languages saying the same thing but
  nobody really understanding?
Control by confusion? Power by puzzlement?
Too complicated for me, dear Friend, and
  quite frankly, such a plan doesn't
  seem quite like you.
No, I think *we* created this vast and
  dangerous concoction of argument
Because we are so clever.
But if we are so clever,
How come we're so stupid?

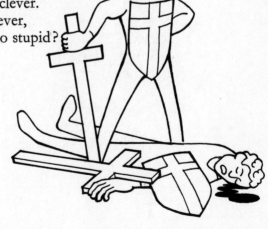

Saying it

Lord – you have a minute? – this is
   about saying it; putting it into words.
People don't, Lord. Not about the one
   thing they should.
About liking someone.
We don't *say* it, Lord; hardly ever.

I'm not talking about love, Lord.
   Lerv, luv. The stuff they use in
   poems and pop songs and movies.
That's got *too* many words. Meaningless.
Once, Lord, I was talking to a very
   powerful rich tycoon sort of man
   who was inclined to walk a bit by
   himself, like me, and as I left him
   I told him, truthfully, that I liked him.
'I like you,' I said. And suddenly his
   eyes were wet.
It was a surprise; a shock; a disturbance.
Oh, a person needs telling, Lord.
It warms a person, Lord.

People don't say it – and the people
   they should say it to shrivel a little
   for want of hearing it – and themselves
   remain silent.

A person needs to hear it, Lord,
To teach him how to say it.
A loving contagion of words, a sort of measles.
You catch it, and give it to others.
Begin the infection, Lord,
and let it grow to epidemic.

Sack of guilt

Lord, this is about guilt.
   That old lying-down-by-night-with and
   rise-up-in-the-morning-with thing, Lord.
You have a minute?
Well, I once read in the paper this
   article where a lady said she, at forty,
   gave up guilt.
She said she'd decided to like herself a little more.
Wise lady. Strong lady. To be admired.
But not easy to do, Lord.

It starts so early, you see, Lord, the guilt.
Often before you can read or write or count to ten.
And kindly teachers, if you're a bit backward

in such things, make you feel a mite
   guilty about it.
And the poison's in. Earlier even; with
   dirty nappies, or not pleasing nanny.

Now, Lord, I'm not a fool.
   Well, no more than most –
And I know full well that feeling bad about doing
   wrong is the main reason for doing right.
And it works. One of your best ideas. Clever.
   We should take more notice.
Well, what I'm on about, Lord,
Is the *clearing up of arrears*.

I'll explain.
A person does a thing against the law, he
   gets caught, he pays the fine or does
   a bit of time and it's done with.
Clean slate; fresh start and so on. Good.
Clearly defined. Over and done with.
But it's the other kind of guilt, Lord.
The odd bits and pieces, which cling together
   and become a bloody great sack on the back.
The arrears.

A heap, a pile, a stinking compost heap
   of regretted actions.
Nowhere to pay a fine; nowhere to do time.
You carry that sack yourself!
And a person doesn't have to be wicked to get a sack.
Anyone can get one. Everyone (pretty nearly)
   has *got* one!

Even nice people, who do nice things.
   (Well, perhaps they do *now,* to empty a
   little the sack they filled earlier.)

Guilt is a fungus, Lord. A sort of rot.
A below-the-surface, vague, itchy thing.
Maybe to do with kindly teachers
   and clean-nappy nannies and
   don't-look-at-your-sister and go-for-a-
   long-walk and take-a-cold-shower-instead.
Maybe to do with take-your-hand-away
   and how-dare-you and what-a-way-
   to-speak-to-your-mother and wait-till-
   your-father-hears-about-this.

Like barnacles, Lord, limpets,
   The little guilts cling on, hard-shelled.
   And are joined by others.
   And a person gets *encrusted*, Lord.
Heavy with it. The bloody great sack.
   Excuse the language, Lord – and
   the mixed metaphors.
But you know what I mean.
Often, Lord, a person does not fully enjoy
   what he likes most to do,
Because of a 'feeling of guilt'.
Seems a shame. Agreed?
No criticism (it would be a liberty) but agreed?
Guilt waters it all down for a person, Lord.

Mind you (how subtle are your ways),
   I know people do good things because of guilt.
   Give money to things; join committees;

create funds; look after their old parents;
start going to church again.
Part of the Master-plan, Lord?
Part of the Scheme?
Good. But allow me to draw your attention
to others, lots of others, who don't do
a damn (pardon) thing except live
half a life feeling sort of . . . you know . . .
a bit . . . difficult to pin down . . . *guilty*.
Encrusted, Lord. Barnacled; manacled.
Watchmen, unpaid, over their heaps
and piles. Sack-weighted.
Necessary, I accept, Lord.
But *so* necessary?

Help me, O Lord, be like the lady in the paper.
Help me be free of the sack.
If not entirely free, to empty it a little?
Help me to like myself a bit more.
I tell you, Lord (confidentially),
One or two people think I'm not so bad.
And on a good day I can also stand me.
But most of the time, Lord,
                              I could weep.

Vanity, vanity

Did I once read somewhere, Lord
   – you have a minute? –
That all is vanity?
Charles Laughton said it in a movie, too,
   quoting someone, surely.
   It's too good a line for a screenwriter.
'Vanity, vanity, all is vanity',
A remarkable thought in every way.

One of the seven deadlies, am I right?
If not, certainly frowned upon, agreed?
'Be not puffed up' – another quote, Lord?
   And no doubt lots of others.
   A person grows up with it.
'Don't be vain', 'Thinks a lot of himself',
'Bit of a peacock' – or the gentle: 'Big 'ead!'

Now, Lord – a minute more? – a thought.
It seems to me, the older I get,
I see that vanity has its place in the
   pattern of things.
Maybe it is part of your pattern of
   things that as we get older we *do* see it.
I understand; I've admired the pattern before.

Yes, it has a place, vanity.

A great *spur* to a person, vanity is.
  It makes a man hold his stomach in,
  and walk tall, and wear a hairpiece,
  and dress a bit too young.
  And buy too many rounds,
  and never miss a mirror.

A great leveller, vanity is.
It can happen to anyone, it can.
  It keeps women young (in a way),
  keeps them caring, if only for themselves.
  Hairdresser instead of lunch;
  dressmaker before anything.
  And never, *never* miss a mirror.

Well, Lord (a moment more, I'm nearly done),
The problem, not a big one, is this.
  If vanity has a place, a time,
  a position in your Pattern of Things,
Show me the right place? *The right time*?
If it's not altogether bad and can help a person,
  it would be nice to do it right.
After all, a person doesn't want to get disliked.

Thy telly

Lord, not that I don't believe that you are
  all-seeing and so on, but I thought I'd
  give you a little progress report on something.
You have a minute? Well, I'll begin.

Lord, since you first made us and gave us voices
  you must have got used to our almost
  ceaseless racket.
'Raising up our voices', 'cries and lamentations',
  'speaking as one' (*that's* a giggle) and so on.
Much referred to in The Book.
All in all, what with our clamours and
  choruses and mighty assemblages, a fairly
  noisy lot.
And the more we multiplied, the noisier we got.
No argument? Agreed? Read on.

Well, Lord, it may have come to your attention
  that over the past few years we've
  quietened down a little.
And over your beautiful world we are
  making less noise. Even the kids.
It's not that we've become gentler, or
  cleverer, or more civilised. We haven't.
It's not that we are more tolerant and
  understanding and kinder. We aren't.

We don't love our neighbour more.
In fact we don't see too much of him.
He's like us; too busy looking at telly.

The Telly, Lord. A word or two; some thoughts.
Can you bear the subject? Please, a moment.
Well, lately (don't laugh, dear Friend) in my
    more fanciful moments, I have seen
    your hand in it.
In the telly.
Not the programmes; not the chat shows nor
    the domestic comedy series nor the old movies
    nor the wrestling nor the Ballroom Dancing
    nor the Racing nor the Searching Looks At
    World Events.
Nor even the Commercials.
No, Lord, I mean in the whole idea of Telly.
Its very existence.

A sort of miracle, I think.
  We watch, as it happens, in full colour,
  men walk on your beautiful moon;
  we see the happenings in other lands, if not at the
  same moment, an hour or two later;
  moments of glory, or tragedy, or idiocy.
We get to know more; our eyes are opened.
  We learn (the quickest way) by seeing.
Plenty wrong with telly; no argument, but
  in the main we are wiser for it.
Which has always been your wish,
  from the Beginning,
That we should be wiser.

So it follows (I think) that your hand is in it.
  If the telly shows us how the other fellow
  lives, and by knowing, we find him a
  bit less strange or frightening or suspicious,
It can't be bad.
  If we are shown people to admire or look
  up to or worth copying,
  if we are privileged to look in upon the
  interplay of fine minds,
It must be good. Agreed?
Am I on to something, Lord?
Have I caught you at it again?

You made us, and we've let you down times
  beyond number.
You gave us sustenance and surrounded us
  with beauty.
You forgave us and rewarded us and
  heaped us with gifts.

You showed us miracles and mighty
  happenings until we took such things
  for granted.
Have you now, dear Creator, given us the
  most risky gift of all,
A mirror? To see ourselves?
The Telly? To see ourselves?

If it is your gift to us, Lord (and pretty well
  everything is),
  help us not muck it up too much.
Forgive us, Lord, for what we've done to it already.
  Forgive us our quiz games and our professional
  wheedlers; our two-minute pundits and
  our lying commercials; our Party Political
  Broadcasts – with their trained-in-sincerity
  speakers.
Pardon us, Lord, our transgressions of taste,
  our love of violence, our preoccupation with sex,
  our worship of idols (both matinee *and* sport), our
  cock-eyed priorities.
We have a long and consistent record of
  foolishness, Lord. Help us, please.
If thy gift of telly was to do us some good,
  give us now the sense to let it.

On liking children

Lord, something on my mind. (What, again?)
You have a minute?
It's about liking children.
One of the great unquestioned generalities.
   The expected broad statement; accepted;
   standard practice: 'I like children.'
Well, Lord, I'm not sure I do.
Some, certainly. But not all.
   And if you answer people's 'You like
   children?' with 'Er – not many', they
   look at you funny and you feel guilty.
Mind you, most everything makes me feel
   guilty (see elsewhere in these pages).

Lord, let me try to explain this.
   Let me say, right away, that I do
   not mind in children the things of childhood.
The noise, the mischief, the inquisitiveness,
   the sauciness and so on.
The honesty, the simplicity, the candour
   and frankness and gaiety.
I can stand it; if they give me a headache
   or get on my nerves I can take an
   aspirin and shut the window.
No, it's not the children children who
   bother me; it's the child grown-ups.

Lord, it may be that in the wondrous
   permutations that are called people,
You decided for some special reason
   to make a few 'full-grown from the
   womb' experiments.
Children who look like children (from
   a little way away) but who are
   grown-ups.
To be grown up is difficult; a person
   needs time. Dangerous stuff; it shouldn't
   be hurried.
Which is why grown-ups below the age of
   say, ten, scare the hell out of me.

I'll be honest; I'm not too fond of most
   full-size grown-ups, but I can handle it.
But when the grown-up qualities I dislike
   gleam and radiate from *children*, I can't.
(There seem to be more and more of these
   children, Lord, ask anyone. Perhaps, in
   nurseries and infant classes, they *breed*. It
   does not seem impossible.)
No, dear Friend, I cannot handle the sophisticated
   roué who has four more years before shaving.
Or the male-appraising gaze of a seven-year-old woman.

There is a purity in childhood, I read somewhere.
Thus it may be that the child grown-ups
   have their grown-up qualities in purer form.
Un-adult-erated in the truest sense!
Pure malevolence, *pure* cynicism, *pure*
   malice, *pure* wickedness.
(I'm not exaggerating, Lord, ask anyone.)

Full-strength power from a smaller than
    normal source *must* be frightening, Lord.
How can I *like* them, Lord?
If it's wrong, if I should try harder to find
    loving tolerance for this miniaturised
    transistorised terrorising breed,
Forgive me, but I can't.

I don't want to worry you, good Friend,
    but these incubi recognise others of
    their own at a glance – and band together.
These mutants join forces; become units.
We real grown-ups are their enemy,
    and are defenceless against their power.
For marvellously simple is their camouflage,
    and brilliant their disguise.
They look exactly like children.
A last thought, Lord. Are they sort of
    rejects? Satan's offspring? Gone-wrong cherubim?
Do you *wonder* I'm scared?

Sam just don't know

This is on behalf of Sam, Lord,
   – you have a minute?
Sam, Lord. Sam? Does he come to mind?
Although, it must be admitted, you
   could mix him up with one or two others.
Not others called Sam; others *like* Sam.

It occurs to me, Lord, that you may *not* know him.
For certainly he doesn't know you.
   Self-made man, Sam.
No help from anyone, as he often says.
Nearly everything he says, he says often.
Believe me, Lord, if you don't know
   him, you're showing a profit.
Self-made bore, Sam.
But still, a word on his behalf.

Sam doesn't *enjoy*, Lord.
He is rich and he doesn't lack a thing.
In fact he's got two of most everything;
Mainly because other people have only got one.
A barricade of possessions, Lord.
But he doesn't enjoy.
   He neither hides behind his barricade,
   Nor stands out in front.
This is a way to *live*, Lord?

A remarkable story, Sam's. Not
    unique, not unusual, but certainly
    deserving of (some) admiration.
Hard-working, tough, courageous, far-sighted,
    shrewd, energetic, dynamic – all
    words used in the *Times* piece about
    him – so it must be true.
Sort of non-Jewish tablets of the Law the
    Times is, Lord (no offence meant).
One or two more words can be used, Lord. Non-*Times*.
    Selfish, blind, bigoted, intolerant,
    pig-headed, unforgiving.
And stupid, Lord.
Self-made stupid Sam.

His sons don't like him, Lord.
    They have reason; I've gone into it.
    No time for them had Sam. Too busy.
Sam made himself – and left out love.
One daughter. Closer to him, but she
    grew discouraged.
No love from Sam; only exacting standards
    and 'Don't-argue-girl'.
She married a plumber, Lord. Two kids.
    Yes, I thought you might know her.
    I agree. *Very* nice.

Sam's wife is sort of shrivelling, Lord.
A tight, on-the-edge look.
    Know what I mean?
Has to remember a long list of
    things not to mention, like
    the boys and the daughter and the grandchildren.

Self-made Sam's lonely missus.
    She drinks a little, Lord, to help wash
    down the pills, to soften the focus a little.
To take away the taste of too many cigarettes.

Yet Sam is not *bad*, Lord.
    All the non-*Times* words, but not *bad*.
    Not kind, not considerate, not loving – nor
    even affectionate.
    Not gentle, not tactful, not pleasant,
    not sympathetic – nor even aware.
It seems to me, Lord,
That Sam just doesn't *know*.

Terrible thing, Lord, to just not know.
A sad, sad thing.
    Imagine, a man can be single-minded
    and eyes-on-target and blinkered and
    determined and dynamic etc. (see *Times* list above),
And make a fortune,
And have two of most everything,
And be so plain *stupid*.
Not uncommon, Lord. Agreed?
Can anything be done?

A last thought. And thank you for listening.
It may be that it is your habit,
    when you hear that someone is
    convinced he made himself ('with no help'),
    to stay away, to leave him to it; to take no action.
It's understandable.
But would you consider,
    In the matter of self-made Sam,

Adding a touch here and there?
Believe me, I don't like him, and he has
    no idea I'm asking you –
But would you consider it?

Jealousy

Lord, something rather serious; big.
You have a minute or two?
It may take more, but the subject will be familiar
   to you and you may have a ready-mixed cure.
It's jealousy, Lord.
Familiar? Cain and Abel? Joseph? Jacob?
   And all the millions since then?

Well, Lord, for a person to know he's one of
   millions, alive and dead, is no help at all. None.
Jealousy narrows a person, Lord.
   Makes his soul smaller; his character meaner.
   Makes him cutting in his words, without trust.
Full of suspicion and very dark thoughts.
Need we have it, Lord?
It may be it's all part of some master plan
   – and believe me, I don't expect to be shown the plan –
But what *good* is it, Lord?
If Cain killed Abel because of jealousy,
Didn't that sort of show something?
Although I read somewhere else – or maybe
   in the same book – that *you* are jealous.
'A jealous God', it said.
You, dear Friend? Jealous?
I don't believe it. You have too busy a life.
   Have too much to look after.

It would interfere with the work too much.
   Because it always does, Lord, it always does.
   It interferes with *everything*.

Need we have it, Lord? What good does it do?
   It proves nothing – and demands much.
   It breeds violence – and creates fear.
It shrivels a person, Lord, makes him less.
It sits on his shoulder like a vulture
   covered in green slime, murmuring lies
   and obscenities, with bad breath.
Who *needs* it, Lord?

It destroys sleep – or provides bad dreams.
   And getting older doesn't seem to help.
True, a person learns to live with his
   character ailments; his flaws.
He learns how to cover up, to perform
   the comedies of behaviour.
But jealousy, Lord, accepts only the
   thinnest cover – and breaks easily through.

I have a nasty feeling, Lord,
That if you were going to change it, you
   would have done so long ago.
After Cain and Abel – or Joseph and his brothers
   – or Jacob and the birthright business.
Looks like we're stuck with jealousy, Lord.
It's a very depressing prospect.

Maybe I shouldn't have mentioned it.
Still, no harm.
Who else can I talk to?

Best not get involved

Lord, I read in the paper the other
    day – you have a minute? –
    about a woman beaten senseless
    by two men across the road from
    a bus queue.
No one crossed the road to help.
They avoided involvement,
    and later, each other's eyes.
Later still, were intelligent and
    accurate (fairly) in their statements to
    the ambulance people and the police.

Involvement, Lord. A person needs
    help on this one.
A person doesn't like to get involved.
The screaming quarrel (with bumps
    and crockery noise) through the
    party wall; the shouts and
    door slam in the flat above.
A person doesn't like to get involved.
    Drunken curses and a baby crying
    two gardens away; the sudden
    frightened scream of a girl from
    a dark field.
'Best not get involved.'

Lord, people get *killed*.
Yet it's very common, Lord, this
    feeling.
Very natural, very ordinary.
Often more to do with tact than cowardice;
    with distaste rather than disinterest.
Early teachings linger.
    'Don't interfere', 'Keep out of it', 'Don't
    take sides', and the mighty: 'Don't
    get involved'.
And people get killed.
Or slowly die of loneliness in bed-sitters.

'What can One do?'
'One doesn't want to say anything . . .'
'One hesitates to offer help. After all,
    man and wife and all that . . .'
'It doesn't do to poke One's nose in.'
And thus, Lord, the world population
    of 'Ones' increases all the time.
Seems to me that your world is full
    of Ones screaming silently for help
    and Ones hesitating to offer any.
After all, One doesn't want to get involved.

A person must be fair, Lord, there
    are involvers. Doctors, hospitals,
    psychiapeople, tranquilliser-makers,
    opiate-issuers, bromide wholesalers,
Bless 'em, they've never been so busy.
A doctor I know, Lord, in a seven-
    partnership practice, using every
    modern system, recently increased
    his time-per-patient average to
    four point seven six minutes.

Some of the happiest people I know, Lord,
    are those who don't mind getting involved.
Admitted, it can go wrong, it
    can blow up in your face, you can
    get *too* involved (there I go again;
    classic 'One-talk'!)
But happy they are, Lord. Without doubt.
That Samaritan story is not there by
    accident; you were making a point.
I would be of their number, please.

Help me not walk by, Lord.
Let me hear the silent cries.
Remove from me the fear of involvement.
Grant me the sort of unfussy compassion
   that can see clearly and understand.
That can deal with poverty and
   not notice its stench and ugliness.
That can help the aged, ignoring
   the vanities and senilities that are
   part of the courage of age.
That can help the young, overlooking
   how daft and irritating they can be.

Help me not walk by, Lord.
A person can make a life's work
   of not getting involved; of
   keeping himself to himself,
And wake up one day, by himself.
He can make a lifelong habit of
   not hearing cries for help
Until all he can hear are his own.
Not clever, Lord, not clever.
Can I go in the urgent tray?

Man of peace

Lord, you have a minute?
This is about a sort of trembling heat I get.
    I keep it to myself, for I've had all
    the jokes about menopausal flushes I want.
    I also keep it to myself, dear Friend, because
    I've worked out what causes it.
It is the violence locked up in me, Lord.
    The war locked up in a man of peace.

A man of peace am I, Lord, who will go to
    considerable lengths to avoid conflict.
There's a lot like me, Lord.
    We see the other feller's point of view, and
    rather than argue, accept it.
    To avoid conflict, to keep the peace.
It's a habit, a way of life, a sort of philosophy.
    Weakness is in it perhaps, and a lack
    of backbone. Compromise also. And peace.

So we agree, and concur, and keep our voices
    down and keep the peace.
And all the disagreement and loud voices and
    unpeaceful non-concurrence we keep locked up.
And so we walk about, we men of peace,
    full of locked-up war, screwed-down violence.

And sometimes, looking no different from
   the outside, I grow hot, and tremble.
For violent would I be, Lord. Even to murder.

Let me make clear right away, Lord, that
   we peaceful ones don't just blow up, as it were.
We don't every now and then *need* to blow up, to
   explode, to uncork, to release, to let loose.
Not at all; gardening, swimming, golf, football-
   match shouting, a drink or two, a little sex,
And all safety valves are safe. All under control.
No, Lord, it is the other one or two things. A minute
   more?

Lord, there are people who batter babies. They
   break their bones and throw them across rooms.
There are people, Lord, who bruise for life the
   minds and bodies of children by sexual assault.
Others, dear Friend, attack the infirm and elderly
   for the savings in the teapot in the corner.
And, Lord, there are the pushers of drugs.
   Oh Friend, I grow hot and my hands shake.

'Tis said you sent your son to teach us to love.
   To revise a little the 'eye for an eye', the
   hard lines of the Sinai Rules. To turn
   the other cheek and so on.
Well, although we crucified him after beating
   him half to death (why do you *bother*
   with us?), certain of his ideas caught on.
But in the matter, Lord, of the foregoing list
   (by no means complete), I would have the old ways.

82

I tremble and burn, and would batter those
who batter, and break *their* bones, and hurl
them from heights.
The sexual assaulters would I castrate and
kick and stake out naked for birds to peck.
The hands that hurt and steal from the old I
would cut off. Me, myself, man of peace.
Which brings us now to the pushers of drugs.

Are these the true slime-spawn of Satan, Lord?
One of the Dark Prince's major victories?
It could be; for, cut down, they grow two more.
Lopped off, those behind move forward – and
those far far behind, within steel walls of
vast and respectable wealth, grow richer.
'Eye for an eye' is somehow pointless here, for the
pusher is often addict himself, selling to
buy, impersonally dragging others into his
own pit. A sort of economics of evil.

Whole police forces cannot stop it. Armies cannot.
Governments are powerless – and other
governments close their eyes, to help balance
the trade figures.
A major victory for the Prince, Lord? The Tempter?
Such a lovely thing, the poppy. Used here
and there in the world to commemorate
those killed off in war, in their best years.
As things have worked out Lord, what is it,
a bloody *joke*?

Humour

Lord – you have a minute? – this is serious.
I want to be serious about being funny.
   Humour, Lord. The sense of.
Not included in the five senses as a rule.
Overlooked; not counted; taken for granted,
Not included in the senses census.
   (Play on words, Lord, ignore it.)
Overlooked, Lord? The sense of *humour*?
   The other five are but the servants
   of the overlooked one!
A touch of Heavenly genius, Lord!
That extra gift, of humour.

Of infinite variety you made us,
Of every shape and colour.
Which would suggest, dear Creator,
upon looking around, that you
   have a pretty solid sense of humour yourself.
You were fair; all shapes
   and colours to have the same
   basic components,
So many arms and legs and so on.
Sound and careful work.
Work of the sixth day.
And you were pleased with your work.
'Good!' you said. And on the next day rested.

I have the feeling, Lord,
That you gave us the humour later.
A modification, to make us behave better.
  For we didn't give you too much joy
  at the beginning, did we?
Or later either for that matter, did we?
  How could you bear us?
Yes, later came the humour.
More bearable, a person with humour,
  I've noticed it myself.
(Humour didn't *evolve*, my scientists; the Sense was
  given.)

Now, Lord, to the point, to be serious.
A thought occurs lately, which
  leaves behind it a little worry.
Mind you, dear Friend, as the years pass,
  many thoughts have a dusting of worry.
No matter; to the point.

Can humour lose power, Lord?
  Can it tire, like the other senses?
  Is it like an optic nerve, or a taste bud,
  or an inner ear, or the wondrous
  parts that feel and smell?
Does it weaken a little, as they can?
Seems reasonable to assume so,
But to me, more worrying, sort of.

Lord, there are no bifocals for the Sense;
  no hearing aid, no wheelchair.
If, Lord (and this is the worry), the
  humour goes, if the Sense weakens,
I'm not sure I can stay the course.
Don't misunderstand me, Lord, I'm
  grateful for every day you give me.
But every day you give me, Lord,
  as I look around, and see a little
  clearer, and understand a little more,
It seems to me, Lord, I need a
  stronger Sense, not a weaker!

Lord, if I am down in your books
  to live long, to be an Elder,
My thanks, believe me, my thanks.
To live is good.
Even to be creaky and hard-of-hearing
  and bi-focal'd and wheelchair'd
  is better than to be dead.
My thanks, dear Friend, my thanks.
Reduce my faculties as you will,
  but if it is no trouble, can I have
  the Sense full-strength, for the full time?

WORDS
FOR
PAUL

Twice in late 1975 the life of David Kossoff's younger son Paul, 25, was saved by the skill of young doctors. In thanksgiving to their skill 'and to the Almighty, who helped also', Kossoff made a decision to give performances of his two famous one-man shows 'without fee, for charity, throughout 1976'. It was announced and the response was enormous. The selection was careful and by early March the tours were organised.

On 19th March, 1976, Paul Kossoff died. 'In America, far from us, but peacefully, without pain, and among friends.' The performances were done as a memorial: 'To a nice young man – and one of the best blues guitarists in the world'. BBC-TV's programme about the year called 'David and Paul' used one of David Kossoff's moving 'Words for Paul'. Many people asked for a copy of the words. They follow, with two other pieces.

All right now

You rest in a peaceful place, my son.
  In a summerhouse, near quiet pools,
  with shady trees, and roses.
It's not quite you, but neither would
  most other last resting places be.
Not much to see; an oaken strip
  with carved lettering picked out in
  black and gold. Most elegant.
Not much to read; your name, your
  opening and closing dates, and the
  title of your million-seller,
'All Right Now'.

How apt now, the words.
You used words well, my son.
  An apt good use of your own
  words, you would agree?
I hope so, for argument between us
  on the matter, would now be, beloved son,
  sadly one-sided.

So sleep easy. None of your old enemies
  knows where you are, or cares.
Quiet pools and shady trees are not their scene.
  Poppies they like; not roses.

They prefer their customers nearly dead only.
  It is their business to keep them so.
No profit in a dead client.

So sleep easy. Sleep in peace. In the sort
  of peace no drug ever gave you.
You are safe, and warm.
  Warmed by the love you left behind you.
So much love, so much.
  You'd be surprised, beloved son.

You'd be surprised, beloved son, how much
  love you inspired; which endures.
For to be honest, you went to little
  trouble for anybody.
Certainly, it must be admitted, you found
  little time for other things either.
Like envy, or malice, or enmity, or prejudice.

A mystery, this legacy of love you left.
  For you didn't put yourself out to create it.
You had no memory for birthdays or anniversaries.
  You didn't write letters or make 'phone calls.
You had no sense of 'duty', of filial or
  familial things. You didn't keep in touch.
A puzzlement, the whole thing.

Humour you had, with a gentle edge.
  Acceptance you had (ah, a clue perhaps).
You accepted people, as they were,
  right'uns and wrong'uns, as they came.
And they were in some way warmed.

And when, so young, you were gone from them,
　　they found love for the giver of warmth.
So many they are, you'd be surprised, beloved son.

Time now to go. To leave this peaceful
　　place of trees and pools and roses.
A thought occurs; to make you smile:
　　Your grandfather, who died long before
　　your birth, was a loving man.
He had time for people. He accepted; he warmed.
Were you him again, beloved son?
　　Briefly visiting?

Late great Paul

That was a night, that show in Croydon.
That was a night!
   You left 'em for dead, you slayed 'em!
Lucky you had a high stage, and big roadies,
   or they would have torn your clothes off.
Worshippers they were, followers, the faithful.
And you played that night, my Paul, to
   show 'em they'd chosen right.

Full value you gave, over and above.
And they rose and shouted and came
   down the aisles like for Billy Graham!
Declaring themselves true to the faith.
Paul: evangelist with a guitar.
Pint-sized powerhouse with a plectrum
   for prayerbook.
That was a night, that Croydon show.

You stood like always, face up to the lights.
Making the faces, the famous grimaces,
   silently screaming the notes you made,
   guitar held low, at arms' length,
   wrestled with, vanquished, shown its master,
On the really bent notes, pulled back hard,
   as though to bend it to match the note.
An ecstasy, an agony, a freedom!

On that night, halfway through, a surprise.
Four sons of Ham, very black, on brass.
To one side, in line, a mike each, on brass.
    Unison-playing to make the hair prickle.
And you, Paul, as though hearing in their
    music the source-spring of your own
    special way, moved across, to join the line.
Big black men, in bright colours, in unison,
With little Paul, in denim, in blood-harmony.

In unison they paused, for sixteen bars,
    and four brothers turned to see their fifth,
Bending notes in solo language their own.
    And four white grins of approval showed.
    Approval, recognition of a natural son of
    the blues. And love.
Then it was their time again, and a great
    great sound began.
Keyboard, drums, bass – and the brothers five in line.

What a finish to a number that was!
What a storm you blew!
Your flock went crazy, saw visions,
    beheld miracles, spoke in voices,
And the stage was full of joy.

And what a finish, later, to the evening,
When they would not let you go.
They stood and they shouted and called your name
Knowing you'd come, and back you came.
With the impish grin, the raised arm, the 'V' sign.
    Keyboard, rhythm and black men on brass.
    All big-built, tall, waiting for the off.

Down front a bit, their pint-sized friend.
  With a joyful face, ready to give encore.

They still talk of that encore, that twenty minutes.
They still talk of that Croydon night.
And for once, no faces, no famous grimaces.
At *us* you looked – and gave off joy like heat.
What an end that was, to a night.

Backstage later, a quieter end, in a
  soft voice, from one of the brothers on brass,
Who had witnessed your joy, and my own.
The eldest he was, called Pete, with
  grey in the tight black wool,
Calm he was, and careful with words.
'You are right,' he said. 'Nobody *is* like
  Paul on guitar, and the reason, you
  understand, is that Paul *is* the guitar.'

A fitting epitaph, beloved son.
But needed too early, late great Paul.

Elegant light brown suit

How handsome you look, how elegant, my Paul,
  in your well-cut light brown pin-striped suit.
How well I remember when you bought it,
  on a Wednesday, Windsor High Street, off the peg.
To you, my Paul, just another suit.
For your mother and me, so much more.
  A symbol of hope, a sign of new life.
Celebration clothes for a given-back son.

For given back you were, my Paul.
  Fought for, by young doctors and tireless
  nurses with swift competent hands.
You died, my Paul. You were dead.
  We will call things by their right names.
  You were dead; and then alive again.
  Gone away, and brought back.
  By doctors and nurses, and God.

Monitor screens and tubes and
  pipes and wires and drugs, and God.
Intensive care techniques and
  ceaseless vigilance and skill, and God.
A tolerant smile you had for Dad,
  with his talk of thanks to God.
But we will call things by their right names,
  and the giver of life is God.

So back with the living you were.
  Model patient, uncomplaining, with
  natural good manners, and humour.
A peasant constitution, from village
  forbears, gave you swift recovery,
And the colour came back, and the mind
  awoke, unimpaired, and the heart, so recently
  still, so silent, beat again strong and true.

By your bed we sat, my Paul, and
  looked at our reborn son, our family miracle.
Soon well enough to celebrate your
  twenty-fifth birthday, in your hospital room,
With loving friends, and cards, and champagne
  – and a cake with *both* your birthdates on.
Our miracle son, soon ready to go home
  – and buy a light brown pin-striped suit.

Soon to go home, soon to re-enter your world and
  life-style where lurked such danger.
Soon to restart habits now doubly perilous,
  soon to ignore the warnings of loving friends.
Soon, perhaps too soon, my peasant-strong
  son, to go up on a stage, with undimmed skill.
  To give joy to your fans, who roared
  a welcome, to their Paul in his new brown suit.

Soon also to be ill and still again, with tubes
  and pipes and monitors, and danger.
Quickly over, quickly home, my peasant Paul.
  Was no terrible warning there, dear son?
Or had you found a place the first time
  that beckoned return; offered peace?

A hard thing to say, but one hears of such things
   – and one should call things by their right names.

Well again, strong again, soon to America,
   Heathrow farewell, in your light brown suit.
Our far-off miracle son, never a one for
   letters home, or wish-you-were-here cards.
From others we gathered news, as of old.
   Of Big Nights, and long studio sessions,
   and hangers-on, and the old dangers.
To God, who gave you back once, we prayed again
   for your safe return.

Did the Good Lord, I wonder, hear and
   give careful thought to what was best?
Did he allow you a glimpse, I wonder,
   that first time, offering you rest?
For bring you home safe to us he certainly did,
   safe and secure and in perfect peace.
Lying down, in an oaken box, satin-lined.
Elegant, in your light brown pin-striped suit.

Different skills have attended you, my Paul,
   My family miracle, my peasant-strong son.
   'As-in-life' practitioners; layers-out;
   preparers of the Departed; men of the tomb.
Very natural you look, my Paul, rather
   serious in sleep. Remote, withdrawn.
Your long hair tidy, your cheeks of good colour,
   Some of which has come off,
   On the wide lapels,
   Of your elegant light brown pin-striped suit.